Awesome Ancie

MW01251563

T. rex Is King

Cretaceous Life

Dougal Dixon

This library edition published in 2014 by Ticktock
First published in the USA in 2013 by Ticktock,
an imprint of Octopus Publishing Group Ltd

Distributed in the USA by Black Rabbit Books
P.O. Box 3263, Mankato, MN 56002

Published and distributed in the UK by Bounty Books a division of
Octopus Publishing Group Ltd

Library of Congress Cataloging-in-Publication Data

Dixon, Dougal.
T. rex Is King: Cretaceous Life / by Dougal Dixon.
p. cm. -- (Awesome Ancient Animals)
Includes index.
Summary: "Describes the animals of the Cretaceous Period when
many types of dinosaurs evolved, including the famous Tyrannosaurus.
Includes an Animal Families glossary, prehistory timeline, and
pronunciation guides"-- Provided by publisher.
Audience: Grades 4-6.

ISBN (US) 978-1-78325-199-5 (hardcover, library bound)
1. Dinosaurs--Juvenile literature. 2. Paleontology--Cretaceous--
Juvenile literature. I. Title.
QE861.5.D662 2013
560'.177--dc23
2012002743

Printed and bound in China
10 9 8 7 6 5 4 3 2

A CIP record for this book is available from the British Library
ISBN (UK): 978 0 75372 808 6

Editor: Margaret Parrish
Designer: Steve West

Contents

Introduction

This map shows how the Earth looked in the Cretaceous Period. The continents were separated, but slowly moving together.

This map shows how the Earth looks today. North and South America are joined together, and Asia is linked to Europe and Africa.

Awesome Ancient Animals follows the evolution of animals.

Earth's history is divided into eras, which are divided into periods. These last millions of years. *T. rex Is King* takes you back to the Cretaceous Period, when many dinosaurs evolved, including the most famous predator of all— *Tyrannosaurus*. Smaller, feathered creatures also appeared.

A LOOK BACK IN TIME

This timeline shows how simple creatures evolved into many differnt and complex life-forms. This took millions and millions of years. In the chart, MYA stands for million years ago.

ERA	BOOK	PERIOD	
CENOZOIC ERA	**THE ICE AGE**	1.81 MYA to now QUATERNARY	This is a time of ice ages and mammals. Our direct relatives, Homo sapiens, appear.
	ANCIENT MAMMALS	65 to 1.81 MYA TERTIARY	Giant mammals and huge, hunting birds rule. Our first human relatives start to evolve.
MESOZOIC ERA	**CRETACEOUS LIFE**	145 to 65 MYA CRETACEOUS	Huge dinosaurs evolve. They die out by the end of this period.
	JURASSIC LIFE	200 to 145 MYA JURASSIC	Large and small dinosaurs and flying creatures develop.
	TRIASSIC LIFE	250 to 200 MYA TRIASSIC	The "Age of Dinosaurs" begins. Early mammals live alongside them.
PALEOZOIC ERA	**EARLY LIFE**	299 to 250 MYA PERMIAN	Sail-backed reptiles start to appear.
		359 to 299 MYA CARBONIFEROUS	The first reptiles appear and tropical forests develop.
		416 to 359 MYA DEVONIAN	Bony fish evolve. Trees and insects come on the scene.
		444 to 416 MYA SILURIAN	Fish with jaws develop and sea animals start living on land.
		488 to 444 MYA ORDOVICIAN	Primitive fish, trilobites, shellfish, and plants evolve.
		542 to 488 MYA CAMBRIAN	First animals with skeletons appear.

Quetzalcoatlus

By the end of the Cretaceous Period, the flying reptiles—the pterosaurs—had become truly enormous. *Quetzalcoatlus* was among the biggest. It had the wingspan of a small airplane, although it didn't weigh much more than an adult man.

Most pterosaurs lived near the water, where they hunted for fish. *Quetzalcoatlus* lived inland. It may have been a scavenger, feeding on the bodies of dead dinosaurs. It would have soared in the skies like a vulture, looking for its next meal.

Animal fact file

NAME: QUETZALCOATLUS (AFTER THE ANCIENT MEXICAN GOD, QUETZALCOATL, WHICH WAS A FLYING SERPENT)

PRONOUNCED: KWETS-UL-COE-AT-LUSS

GROUP: PTEROSAURS

WHERE IT LIVED: TEXAS

WHEN IT LIVED: LATE CRETACEOUS PERIOD (84 TO 65 MILLION YEARS AGO)

WINGSPAN: 35 FT (10.6 M)

SPECIAL FEATURES: BROAD WINGS, LONG NECK, VERY LONG JAWS

FOOD: POSSIBLY CARRION

MAIN ENEMY: NONE

DID YOU KNOW?: TODAY, THE BIRD WITH THE LARGEST WINGSPAN IS THE ALBATROSS, AT 11 FT (3.3 M).

A complete skeleton of *Quetzalcoatlus* has not been found. We know how it looked from fossils that have been found and pieced together.

Elasmosaurus

The plesiosaurs were swimming reptiles, and most had very long necks. *Elasmosaurus* had a neck that was 25 ft (7.5 m) long—more than half its total length. It cruised the ocean off North America at the end of the Cretaceous Period, hunting fish that were in great supply.

The way the vertebrae of its neck were formed suggests that *Elasmosaurus* swam near the water's surface and reached down to snatch its prey.

Elasmosaurus had tiny nostrils but they were not used for breathing. They helped it sense prey moving in the water. To breathe, *Elasmosaurus* came to the surface and breathed through its mouth.

Animal fact file

NAME: ELASMOSAURUS (THIN PLATE LIZARD)

PRONOUNCED: EL-LAZZ-MOE-SORE-US

GROUP: PLESIOSAURS

WHERE IT LIVED: KANSAS

WHEN IT LIVED: LATE CRETACEOUS PERIOD (84 TO 65 MILLION YEARS AGO)

LENGTH: 42 FT 6 IN (13 M)

SPECIAL FEATURES: LONG NECK WITH 71 VERTEBRAE (HUMANS HAVE JUST 7)

FOOD: FISH

MAIN ENEMY: BIG SWIMMING REPTILES LIKE TYLOSAURUS

DID YOU KNOW?: THE FIRST SCIENTIST TO STUDY ELASMOSAURUS GOT IT BACKWARD. HE THOUGHT THE TAIL WAS THE NECK AND THE NECK WAS THE TAIL.

Tylosaurus

Tylosaurus was one of the biggest and fiercest of the mosasaurs—giant lizards who evolved to swim. By the Late Cretaceous Period, ichthyosaurs (the main sea hunters of the Jurassic) were extinct. The mosasaurs evolved in their place, eating the same food and hunting the same way.

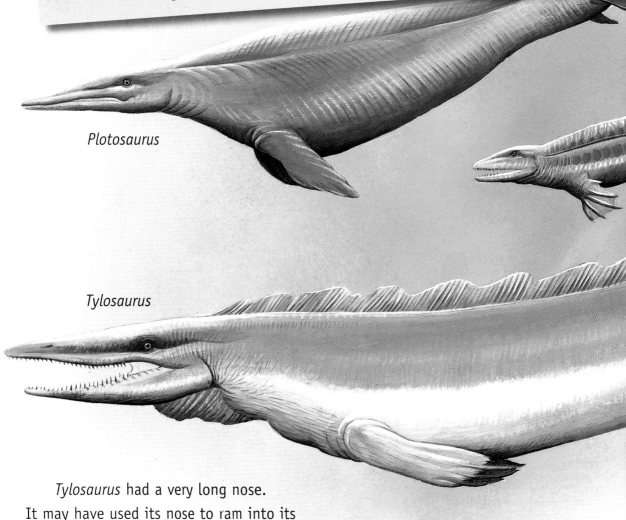

Plotosaurus

Tylosaurus

Tylosaurus had a very long nose. It may have used its nose to ram into its prey, stunning it before eating it.

Tylosaurus had joined toes that formed a paddle. It used its flat tail to push itself through the water with powerful sideways strokes.

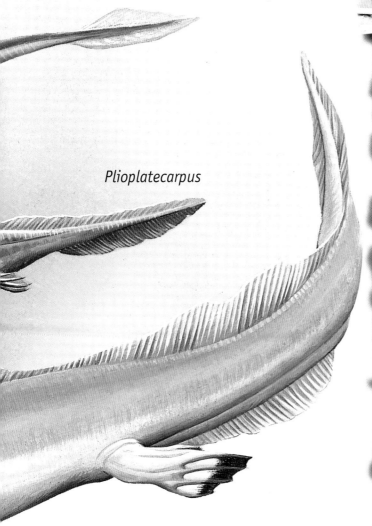

Plioplatecarpus

Animal fact file

NAME: TYLOSAURUS (RAM LIZARD)

PRONOUNCED: TIE-LOW-SORE-US

GROUP: MOSASAURS

WHERE IT LIVED: KANSAS

WHEN IT LIVED: LATE CRETACEOUS PERIOD (84 TO 65 MILLION YEARS AGO)

LENGTH: 30 FT (9 M)

SPECIAL FEATURES: LONG BODY, PADDLELIKE LIMBS, SHARP TEETH, AND A RAMMING POINT ON THE NOSE

FOOD: FISH, AMMONITES AND OTHER SEA REPTILES

MAIN ENEMY: NONE

DID YOU KNOW?: TYLOSAURUS WAS NAMED RHINOSAURUS WHEN IT WAS FOUND. THIS WAS ALREADY THE NAME OF A MODERN LIZARD, SO ITS NAME WAS CHANGED.

Iguanodon

Iguanodon was one of the first dinosaurs to be discovered. Scientists studying it thought that it looked like a big reptile. Most big reptiles are meat-eaters, but the teeth of this fossil showed it ate plants. The iguana, a plant-eating lizard, has similar teeth. So the plant-eating dinosaur was named Iguanodon—"iguana tooth."

Scientists first thought that *Iguanodon* stood upright, resting on its tail like a kangaroo. Now they think it walked on all fours, only reaching up to feed.

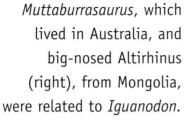

Muttaburrasaurus, which lived in Australia, and big-nosed *Altirhinus* (right), from Mongolia, were related to *Iguanodon*.

Animal fact file

NAME: IGUANODON (IGUANA TOOTH)

PRONOUNCED: IG-GWAH-NO-DON

GROUP: ORNITHOPOD DINOSAURS

WHERE IT LIVED: NORTHERN EUROPE

WHEN IT LIVED: EARLY CRETACEOUS PERIOD (135 TO 125 MILLION YEARS AGO)

LENGTH: 30 FT (9 M)

SPECIAL FEATURES: FINGER SPIKE USED FOR DEFENSE AND FOR RIPPING TREES

FOOD: PLANTS

MAIN ENEMY: BIG MEAT-EATING DINOSAURS, LIKE NEOVENATOR

DID YOU KNOW?: IGUANODON'S FIFTH FINGER WAS SMALL AND FLEXIBLE AND USED LIKE A THUMB.

Olorotitan

The duckbills were the main plant-eaters at the end of the Cretaceous Period. They are called duckbills because their mouths looked like a duck's beak. The beak was used to strip needles from trees. Duckbills had massive chewing teeth that could grind the toughest plant material.

Scientists think the duckbills lived in groups and laid their eggs in nests. Young dinosaurs would have stayed in the herd until they were adults.

Head crests were often hollow and used to make signaling noises. Each shape of crest made a different noise, so herds would have been able to tell each other apart.

Animal fact file

NAME: OLOROTITAN (GIANT SWAN)

PRONOUNCED: OH-LOW-ROW-TIE-TAN

GROUP: ORNITHOPOD DINOSAURS

WHERE IT LIVED: RUSSIA

WHEN IT LIVED: LATE CRETACEOUS PERIOD (70 TO 65 MILLION YEARS AGO)

LENGTH: 30 FT (9 M)

SPECIAL FEATURES: STRANGELY SHAPED CREST ON THE HEAD

FOOD: TWIGS, LEAVES AND CONIFER NEEDLES

MAIN ENEMY: BIG MEAT-EATING DINOSAURS LIKE TYRANNOSAURUS

DID YOU KNOW?: OLOROTITAN WAS NAMED FOR ITS LONG AND SWANLIKE NECK.

Tarchia

The ankylosaurs were the most heavily armored group of animal to exist. Their backs were tightly packed with armor plates that made them as tough as tanks. They were also armed—some with spikes and others with clubs on their tails. *Tarchia* had a tail club.

Tarchia could swing its solid-bone tail club with great force. Any meat-eating dinosaur attacking it risked having its legs broken by the club.

Tarchia means "brainy" and this dinosaur had a bigger braincase than other ankylosaurs. Despite its name, it was not very intelligent.

Animal fact file

NAME: TARCHIA (BRAINY)

PRONOUNCED: TAR-KEE-A

GROUP: THYREOPHORAN DINOSAURS

WHERE IT LIVED: ASIA

WHEN IT LIVED: LATE CRETACEOUS PERIOD (78 TO 69 MILLION YEARS AGO)

LENGTH: 20 FT (6 M)

SPECIAL FEATURES: BACK COVERED IN ARMOR, CLUB ON THE END OF ITS TAIL

FOOD: LOW-GROWING PLANTS

MAIN ENEMY: BIG MEAT-EATING DINOSAURS LIKE TYRANNOSAURUS

DID YOU KNOW?: VERTEBRAE IN THE TAIL WERE FUSED, ALLOWING IT TO SWING ITS CLUB.

Stygimoloch

At the end of the Cretaceous Period, a group of dinosaurs called the marginocephalians appeared. One group of marginocephalians was the boneheads. These goat-sized animals had a massive lump of bone on their heads that they used like a battering ram. One of the strangest-looking boneheads was *Stygimoloch*.

Stygimoloch had a spectacular number of horns around its skull. These made it look bigger and fiercer than it actually was.

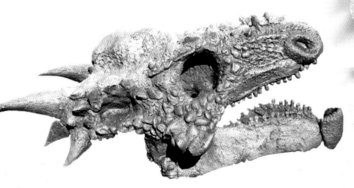

The skulls of the marginocephalians were so solid that they are frequently found as fossils, even though the rest of the skeleton has disappeared.

Animal fact file

NAME: STYGIMOLOCH (HORNED DEVIL FROM THE RIVER OF DEATH)

PRONOUNCED: STIH-GEE-MOLE-LOCK

GROUP: MARGINOCEPHALIANS

WHERE IT LIVED: CANADA AND THE MIDWESTERN UNITED STATES

WHEN IT LIVED: LATE CRETACEOUS PERIOD (71 TO 65 MILLION YEARS AGO)

LENGTH: 9 FT (2.7 M)

SPECIAL FEATURES: THE STIFF, STRAIGHT TAIL USED FOR BALANCE

FOOD: PLANTS

MAIN ENEMY: BIG MEAT-EATING DINOSAURS LIKE TYRANNOSAURUS

DID YOU KNOW?: ALL BONEHEADS USED THEIR HEAVY HEADS TO HEAD-BUTT RIVALS.

Triceratops

Triceratops is one of the most recognizable of the dinosaurs. It had a huge rhinoceros-like body and a massive bony head with three horns pointing forward. It roamed the plains of North America in herds at the very end of the Age of Dinosaurs.

Triceratops used its big beak to snip off twigs from bushes and trees. It had heavy chopping teeth and cheek pouches that held food while it chewed.

Triceratops was a ceratopsian dinosaur. All ceratopsian dinosaurs looked similar, except for the number and arrangement of horns. Some had a single nose horn, some had a pair of horns over the eyes, and some had horns on their armored neck shields.

Animal fact file

NAME: TRICERATOPS (THREE-HORNED FACE)

PRONOUNCED: TRY-SERRA-TOPS

GROUP: MARGINOCEPHALIANS (CERATOPSIAN GROUP)

WHERE IT LIVED: NORTH AMERICA

WHEN IT LIVED: LATE CRETACEOUS PERIOD (72 TO 65 MILLION YEARS AGO)

LENGTH: 25 FT (7.5 M)

SPECIAL FEATURES: ARMORED NECK SHIELD

FOOD: TOUGH PLANTS

MAIN ENEMY: BIG MEAT-EATING DINOSAURS LIKE TYRANNOSAURUS

DID YOU KNOW?: TRICERATOPS WAS ONE OF THE LAST DINOSAURS TO APPEAR BEFORE ALL DINOSAURS BECAME EXTINCT 65 MILLION YEARS AGO.

Suchomimus

This frightening creature belongs to a group of dinosaurs called the spinosaurids. These fish-eaters lived in the Cretaceous Period. *Suchomimus* used its claws to hook fish in water and throw them on land, before snapping them up in its long jaws.

Suchomimus was a fierce predator, but it sometimes became the prey. In this picture, a gigantic crocodile lunges out of the water to attack Suchomimus.

Suchomimus had a long, powerful snout and a mouthful of sharp teeth. These allowed it to grasp hold of slippery fish.

Animal fact file

NAME: SUCHOMIMUS (CROCODILE MIMIC)

PRONOUNCED: SOO-KO-MIME-US

GROUP: THEROPODS

WHERE IT LIVED: NORTH AFRICA

WHEN IT LIVED: EARLY CRETACEOUS PERIOD (110 TO 100 MILLION YEARS AGO)

LENGTH: 36 FT (11 M)

SPECIAL FEATURES: LONG NARROW JAWS LIKE A CROCODILE'S

FOOD: FISH

MAIN ENEMY: A GIGANTIC CROCODILE CALLED SARCOSUCHUS

DID YOU KNOW?: THE SPINOSAURIDS WERE WIDESPREAD. RELATED DINOSAURS HAVE BEEN FOUND IN ENGLAND, THAILAND, AND BRAZIL.

Buitreraptor

Scientists used to think that the small, fast, meat-eating dinosaurs that looked like birds lived only in Europe, Africa, and North America. Then, in 2005, the remains of *Buitreraptor* were found in South America. In the Cretaceous Period, South America was an island, like Australia is today. The ancestors of *Buitreraptor* and other birdlike dinosaurs must have existed before the continents broke up, perhaps 200 million years ago.

Buitreraptor most likely had feathers. Its long legs and light build show that it was active and probably warm-blooded. Most warm-blooded animals have fur or feathers to keep them warm. Relatives of *Buitreraptor* had feathers.

Several skeletons of *Buitreraptor* were found in the same area of South America. It was probably a common animal. Scientists have built a complete skeleton from the many remains.

Animal fact file

NAME: BUITRERAPTOR (VULTURE HUNTER)

PRONOUNCED: BWEE-TREE-RAP-TER

GROUP: THEROPODS

WHERE IT LIVED: ARGENTINA

WHEN IT LIVED: LATE CRETACEOUS PERIOD OF THE MESOZOIC ERA (90 MILLION YEARS AGO)

LENGTH: 4 FT (1.2 M), MOST OF WHICH WAS TAIL AND NECK. IT WAS THE SIZE OF A CHICKEN

SPECIAL FEATURES: A BIRDLIKE DINOSAUR WITH FEATHERS, LONG LEGS, WINGLIKE LIMBS AND A BEAKLIKE SNOUT. IT HAD FEWER TEETH THAN OTHER MEAT-EATERS

FOOD: SMALL ANIMALS

MAIN ENEMY: BIGGER MEAT-EATERS

DID YOU KNOW?: THE LONG, NARROW JAWS AND SMALL TEETH SUGGEST THAT BUITRERAPTOR HUNTED IN BURROWS FOR SNAKES. SCIENTISTS FOUND FOSSILS OF SNAKES AT THE BUITRERAPTOR SITE.

Deinonychus

Is it a bird? Is it a dinosaur? In the Cretaceous Period, some of the more active meat-eating dinosaurs were so birdlike that it is difficult to decide if they were birds or dinosaurs. *Deinonychus* was one of the most birdlike.

Deinonychus did not fly—its arms were too small to support wings. It had a heavy head, toothy jaws, and a long, stiff tail to balance it as it ran.

The bones of *Deinonychus* were lightweight and hollow, just like a bird's. It had strong muscles for running and jumping. It was clearly very active, which means it was probably warm-blooded. *Deinonychus* may have had a feathery coat.

Animal fact file

NAME: DEINONYCHUS (TERRIBLE CLAW)

PRONOUNCED: DYE-NON-EE-CUSS

GROUP: THEROPODS

WHERE IT LIVED: WESTERN UNITED STATES

WHEN IT LIVED: MIDDLE CRETACEOUS PERIOD (110 TO 100 MILLION YEARS AGO)

LENGTH: 10 FT (3 M), INCLUDING TAIL

SPECIAL FEATURES: BIG CLAW, 5 IN (12 CM) LONG, FOR SLASHING PREY

FOOD: OTHER DINOSAURS

MAIN ENEMY: NONE

DID YOU KNOW?: SEVERAL FOSSILS OF DEINONYCHUS HAVE BEEN FOUND SURROUNDING A BIG PLANT-EATER. THEY MUST HAVE HUNTED IN PACKS.

Tyrannosaurus

Since its discovery about a hundred years ago, *Tyrannosaurus* has been considered as one of the fiercest dinosaurs that ever lived. Weighing over six tons, *Tyrannosaurus* would have been an unstoppable force once it went on the attack.

Tyrannosaurus was a fearsome hunter. The remains of duckbills have been discovered with chunks torn out of them—in the exact shape of *Tyrannosaurus's* mouth. Fossilized *Tyrannosaurus* dung has been found, full of crunched-up bones from huge plant-eaters.

Tyrannosaurus walked on two legs with its back horizontal. Its massive jaws and killing teeth were thrust forward, and its body was balanced by a heavy tail. This is how the terror of the last dinosaurs stalked its prey.

Animal fact file

NAME: TYRANNOSAURUS (TYRANT LIZARD)

PRONOUNCED: TIE-RAN-OH-SORE-US

GROUP: THEROPODS

WHERE IT LIVED: CANADA AND THE WESTERN UNITED STATES

WHEN IT LIVED: LATE CRETACEOUS PERIOD (85 TO 65 MILLION YEARS AGO)

LENGTH: 40 FT (12 M)

SPECIAL FEATURES: HUGE HEAD WITH FORWARD-POINTING EYES; TINY ARMS

FOOD: OTHER DINOSAURS— ESPECIALLY DUCKBILLS

MAIN ENEMY: NONE

DID YOU KNOW?: TYRANNOSAURUS MAY HAVE BEEN A SCAVENGER AS WELL AS A HUNTER.

Animal Families Glossary

Ammonites—a group of sea-dwelling cephalopods common in dinosaur times. They were like squid but in coiled shells, and the shells of each species were all different from one another. Many can be found as fossils today.

Cephalopods—literally the "head-footed" animals. The modern types—the octopus and squid—appear to have legs branching from their faces. In prehistoric times many of them had chambered shells.

Ichthyosaurs—a group of sea-going reptiles. They were adapted to living in the ocean and looked like dolphins or sharks. They had fins on the tail and back and paddles for limbs. Ichthyosaurs were common in the Triassic and the Jurassic periods but died out in the Cretaceous.

Marginocephalians—the plant-eating dinosaurs group that had ornamented heads. The ornaments were sometimes horns and neck shields, and sometimes were domes of bone used as battering rams.

Mosasaurs—a group of sea reptiles from the Late Cretaceous Period. They were very much like swimming lizards with paddles instead of feet. They were very closely related to the monitor lizards of today.

Ornithopods—the plant-eating dinosaurs group that usually walked on two legs. They were present throughout the Late Triassic and Jurassic periods but it was in the later Cretaceous that they became really important.

Plesiosaurs—the group of swimming reptiles with the paddle-shaped limbs and flat bodies. There were two types—the long-necked type and the whalelike, short-necked type. They lived throughout the Age of Dinosaurs.

Pterosaurs—the flying reptiles of the Age of Dinosaurs. They had broad leathery wings supported on a long fourth finger and were covered in hair to keep them warm.

Spinosaurids—type of theropod dinosaurs.

Theropods—the meat-eating dinosaur group. They all had the same shape: long jaws with sharp teeth, strong hind legs, smaller front legs with clawed hands, and a small body balanced by a long tail.

Thyreophorans—the armored dinosaur group. There were two main lines. The first to develop were the plated stegosaurs. The armor-covered ankylosaurs came later.

Glossary

Adapted—changing to survive in a particular habitat or weather conditions.

Ancestor—an early form of the animal group that lived in the past.

Carnivore—a meat-eating animal.

Carrion—meat from a dead animal.

Ceratopsian dinosaur—a type of dinosaur that had frills, spikes and horns as protection.

Cold-blooded—animals, such as reptiles or amphibians, that rely on their environment to control their body temperature.

Conifer—an evergreen tree such as a fir or pine.

Continent—one of the world's main land masses, such as Africa and Europe.

Duckbill—a type of dinosaur that had a beak that looked like a duck's beak or bill.

Evolution—changes or developments that happen to all forms of life over millions of years, as a result of changes in the environment.

Evolve—to change or develop.

Extinct—an animal group that no longer exists.

Flexible—able to twist and turn easily.

Fossil—the remains of a prehistoric plant or animal that has been buried for a long time and become hardened in rock.

Open plain—a wide space without trees.

Ornithopod—a type of plant-eating dinosaur.

Plesiosaur—a reptile that lived in the sea.

Prehistory—a time before humans appeared.

Prey—animals that are hunted by other animals as food.

Primitive—a very early stage in the development of a species.

Reptile—a cold-blooded, crawling or creeping animals with a backbone.

Scavenger—an animal that feeds off food other animals have hunted.

Snout—an animal's nose.

Soared—flew high in the sky.

Vertebrae—small bones that form the spine.

Wingspan—the length of a bird's wings, from the tip of one to the tip of the other.

Index

Picture credits

Main image: 10-11, 20-21 Simon Mendez; 6-7, 8-9, 12-13, 14-15, 16-17, 18-19, 22-23, 24-25, 26-27, 28-29 Luis Rey 42TL, 4TR, 5 (Cenozoic Era), 7, 9, 11, 18, 21, 22, 29 Ticktock Media archive; 5 (Mesozoic Era top, Paleozoic Era top) Simon Mendez; 5 (Mesozoic Era center, Paleozoic Era bottom) Luis Rey; 5 (Mesozoic Era bottom) Lisa Alderson; 15 Chris Tomlin; 13, 16 Gondwana Studios; 25 The Field Museum

Every effort has been made to trace the copyright holders and we apologize in advance for any unintentional omissions. We would be pleased to insert the appropriate acknowledgment in any subsequent edition of this publication.